CEREMONY
FOR
MINNECONJOUX

The publication of this volume is supported in part by a grant from the Kentucky Arts Council with funds from the National Endowment for the Arts.

CEREMONY
FOR
MINNECONJOUX

**Poems by
Brenda Marie Osbey**

Volume Two
in the Callaloo Poetry Series
Published at the University of Kentucky
Lexington, 1983

ISBN: 0-912759-03-8

CALLALOO POETRY SERIES
University of Kentucky
Lexington, Kentucky 40506-0027

In Memory of Alberta Cobb Hamilton
and Sarai Payne
and to Lois Emelda Hamilton

Etching by Colette Delacroix

CONTENTS

1.

my name is felicity
i live inside the city
i am telling only
as much as you can bear

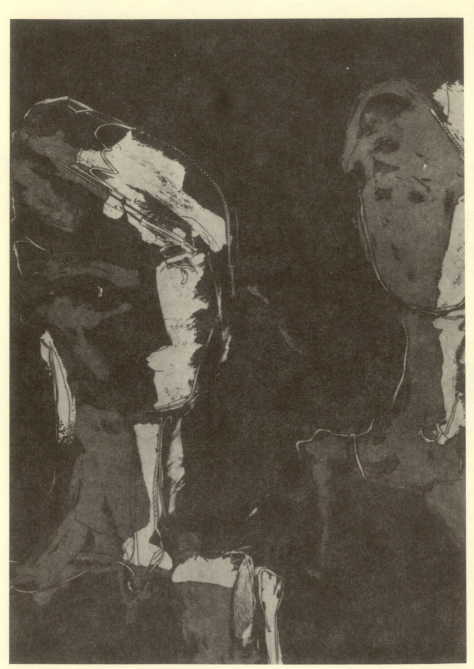

Etching by Colette Delacroix

MADHOUSES

1.
these women mean business
burn their hair only on the ends
and spit tobacco
in the reverend's hedges
they call themselves
mothers
and wear bare feet in public
daring fathers and brothers
to come down on the bankette
and i have seen them dancing
along the interstate in mid-January

we call them madhouses
but it is only that we fear
i know their secrets
only through having learned them
the hardest way

my name is felicity
i live inside the city
i am telling only
as much as you can bear

2.
the bahalia women are coming
from round st. james
carrying the bamba-root in their hands
believe on those hands
and they will see you through seasons
of drought and flood
believe on these hands
and you will cross the grandy-water

3.
journey with me and see what i see

first you hear the leaves
past silence
hitting the ground
moving along the streets
with an undercurrent of rhythm
moving to your bloodbeat
and the sounds of your hands
reaching
reaching up

4.
just before you see them
there is their confounded
jingling
the sound of those root ends
against their tambourines
but no one really hears them coming
just the thud of those bare feet
against the broken surfaces
of the bankette
the low rumbling of song
and then bahalia
bahalia
and yet
you can never say you heard them

it is like that
their coming

5.
it is not tonight i will find the path
i'm ready, damballah
but the way is barred

a slender woman in red skirts
tignon and golden hoops through her ears
young and smooth
and jerking to the sound
of old blood
and thin-skinned men
walking on the graves of the old ones

i am ready, oh spirit
but the way is dark

6.
and like rising from a dream
they are gone
and like a vision they never leave you

standing in my sidelight
you can see them
women so far gone
that their walking is dance
madhouses so grey
against the other houses and churches
that you pretend for now
you do not see them
and never did

but when you make the final journey
and stand at the crossing
seeking the barred footing
it was i who first showed you
and remember my name
it was felicity who told you
how to exit one madhouse
and enter the other

CEREMONY FOR MINNECONJOUX

it was years back you know
down bayou la fouche
she named her daughter
minneconjoux
so that people would not mistake
her indian blood

it was just a lean-to
right up against the water's edge
she said herself
that he would take her out in the damp
never inside
that's what she called it
taking her
she said when they did it out there
his two black greasy plaits
brushing her shoulders
his chest up
away from her
so he could smile down on her
it was not so far
from the slavery her grandmother
had raised her on
a creole woman
fanning herself
recording with her eyes
what happened to the other women
on le compte's land

it was 1943
he came
mostly just passing
in and out the neighborhood
looking just like a mardi gras indian
from off dumaine st.
that's what everyone said he was
until mama lou
called him up the front walk
and asked him what he was
and where he belonged to
he was a choctaw man
but mama lou says
she knew choctaws to be squat
and ducky
she told him about
l'il miz lincoln
with the choctaw blood in her
he repeated it
he was a choctaw man
this time adding
full-blooded
and picking at his teeth
with a sliver
of van-van she had growing
out there.
next day
he was up on the porch
conversing with mama lou
about hard-to-find-work
and low-down-white-folks.

soon after the season broke
he come to work for mama lou
that's when lenazette saw him
for the first time
he wasn't much lighter than her
with two plaits
and a woven head-band.
she come through the run-down page fence gate
and looked up at him on the ladder
what the hell was he doing
she meant to know?
he smiled
mama lou had hired him to fix up.
her face got evil when she asked him
who?
miz philemon he said this time
lenazette went up them stairs
and slammed the door
hard.

lenazette had just finished
from old madame markham's school
that winter he was
walking the streets
looking like a mardi gras
she was sixteen
and wore her hair in french braids
in two buns
on the sides of her head
that spring
he was fixing the windows one day
it was warm
lenazette was at the dresser
about to turn up her hair
when he called in for water
she brought it
not bothering to cover up
the white cotton slip she wore
when she leaned out
she said he could have tea
it had been on ice since last evening
he said
just water
he stood on that ladder
staring down at her slip straps
and again at her braids
i want to touch them
sometime
was what he said
she looked at him
your hands are dirty
he drank the water straight down
they can be cleaned

without much difficulty
he said.

mama lou paid him every week
and fed him once a day
i was to bring him water
when he asked
it began to be sticky
around the house
i wore a white cotton slip
and an eyelet bed jacket
i wore my braids down now
connected together at the ends
i have always liked things
connected together at the ends
after a while
we could talk
he knew french
i still spoke patois
despite mrs. markham's switchings
he understood me
but could only answer in french
that was the first thing
i learned from him.

one day
out on the back porch
i had these culottes on
and a white blouse
he'd come around for water
more than water
he said that mama had told him
about her mama
and le compte's place
we talked about that
about how me and mama
come to look like we did
and how i could go to markham's
but mostly we talked about slaves

and stolen land
he said the food was real good
i told him mama did the cooking
he said to let him comb my hair
i said it was already combed
he undid it without my say-so
i don't know how much mama heard
but when i looked up
she was watching him combing in my hair
when she called me in
i told her he didn't mean no harm
she looked out past me and said
i ain't told you a damn thing about harm
girl
not a god damn thing
days later
when i walked up on them talking
they hushed up

in june
i went with him to bayou la fouche
i sat sewing
while he built the house around me
when i asked how come we just had one room
he told me what-all we had to
we could do there
i was sewing dresses
there was ceremony
holding hands
down on our knees at the water
for weeks i waited
he never touched me
until that one-room was finished
after i lost the first child
he never touched me for six months
not like that anyhow
every night he'd take down my hair
and comb in it
that's when we started going outside

and that's how you come
when i let him
start to combing in my hair again.
he would look down on me
two oily plaits
slapping my neck
and shoulders
i would try not to look

mostly he worked the riverfront
bringing home crates of fruit
vegetables
he never would eat rice
till he saw me feeding it to you

in the evenings
or sometimes early in the morning
before day
he would pull me by the hand

and lead me out to the sycamore tree
he'd just hold onto me
with his arms up on my shoulders
then we'd be down in the grass
and i could see his eyes
i used to tell him you might see
he said one day you would
when i reached up
i knew he was forcing me
making me need what i didn't want
and i started waiting for him to come
and start to combing in my hair
i would hear him mumbling
but i didn't want to know
didn't want to understand
what he was saying
i told him to stop it
and he wouldn't
i tried to move from under him
but his legs pinned me down

he was smiling
and mumbling
and making sounds
and when i saw you in the door
i told him to stop
and he wouldn't
and i picked up a stone
and beat him in his head

when i was ten
i left mama zette
to go live in the city
with mama lou
she had fine smooth hands
and she oiled my hair
when i was twelve
she cut it off
i asked her if it was because
that peterson boy climbed the fence

to talk to me
and put his hands in my hair
i asked her if it was because
my papa sat up on top my mama
holding on her braids
that's when she slapped me
i remember her face
when she slapped me
when she died
she told me mama
had been in charity
then jackson
i looked for papa
up at the bayou
la fouche was empty
the lean-to was not even locked
i found a woman there
her body nothing more
than a cedar switch
i have her picture now

on my bureau
she spoke low
sitting on the floor
sewing dresses
talking of child-having
and other ceremonies

i am minneconjoux
i live in the house on st. claude st.
i connect myself
to the used thing
i keep on my bureau
at mardi gras time
i stand on the walk-way
and watch the indians
dancing off dumaine.

THE FACTORY POEM

i don't want to whisper
somehow when i talk of feelings
some gut
seems to jump into what i say
all up in my mouth
making me wish
i had never learned to speak
remembering nunnie saying
"free yourself
clear yourself"
what did she know of freedom,
chained to some memory
of a man dead twenty or so years ago?
then again
what did she know of being down in mind
all those years
he was still singing "danny boy"
inside her head
all this time
a dead man moving around
inside her body
and her whispering to him
whenever she thought no one could hear.

i heard.
i learned love after she left
or that i'd learned it then
and just not known
because i hadn't put it to use
but i heard
and i don't want to whisper
to a man who's not there.

woman
i said i heard you
heard you had trouble in the mind
woman i heard it takes a man
to make a woman do suicide.

they used to sing it in the factory.

you have taken my keys
all the doors and windows
sing wind and rain songs
i used once to be
an airtight tunnel
complete in myself
thinking i had known
my own limits
you taught me the meaning
of words like
infinite
though once
i lived here also
now i inhabit
an empty hall
that you once made into a mansion
my furnishings are all gone
i have been drained of myself
on warm winter days
i resort to a violence
that teaches you the meaning
of words like
hurt.

what do you know of such things
i live in a factory
where other women also
manufacture blues.

i said i heard you
heard you had trouble in mind
yes i heard you
woman
i done heard you mind.

what do you know of such things
i carry dead things in me
songs and photographs
and dead flowers
i carry sand and seashells
bits of confetti,
eggshells and scribbled note paper
what do you know of such things
with all your doors and windows
sealed so neatly
against the ice and air
what do you know of whispering
inside a room with no ears at all
whispering to thin air
whispering among factory women
telling what mind really means
what do you know of seashells
and dead things
and tunnels?

and what on earth
do i know of you?

MS. LIVVY'S BOY

when jeremiah waters built that brick wall
around ms. livvy's backyard
she was already three years in the ground
it was just a short fence really
and when he stood on the back porch
the neighbor ladies could wave their hands good
    evening
and not feel disrespected
sometimes he would spade up weeds
scrape them out of the parquet
make that nasty sound
metal on brick
he never sang
never talked to himself
and nobody expected ms. livvy's boy to turn so
how could we know
what he would come to?

LETTERS TO BRASIL

dearest brasil
i am writing you this
from ms. livvy's walled-in garden
i left today
and came straight here
all day i have been thinking
whether to cut away the ginger
or leave it be
ms. livvy i'm sure
would not care
one way or the other
if she still lived.

dearest brasil
papa jac is alright
a little shook up some days
but then i am mostly rattled myself
he drinks soup
and sits looking at the radio
i eat cold trout and coffee
and read the daily horoscope
we are quite a pair
you would appreciate the symmetry
if only you could recognize it.

dear brasil
jeremiah has gone to toying with that crokersack
he knows he scares the neighbor ladies
last night i had to ask him
to stop asking mrs. gumble about that old tree
he sees she's nervous
he must know what she's telling them all
of course he doesn't care
neither do i to tell the truth
and so much of it is my doing i feel
i was the one told him

to take off like so
i was the one who said
i want to see you underneath
i want to see the way your juices are made
the part you mixed in the mortar
when you bricked up that wall
he is quite beautiful this way you know
he is like a dancer
where no one has heard music
and at dusk
he takes a near-sacred look
around the forehead
and temples
do you think it is sinful
to unleash such passion?

my sweet brasil
jeremiah brought me plum pudding tonight
do not ask where he got it
it came in a little pound can
with a blue goose strutting before a fireplace
i marvelled over the container a long time
he opened it for me
and we each had two servings
with coffee.

dearest brasil
the neighbors are beginning to ask about me
papa jac tells them anything
anything at all
he is a sweet old pickle
and lets me keep stationery
in one of his king edward cigar boxes.

dear brasil
jeremiah's hands are crepe myrtle bark
he hums these tunes he swears actually exist
some evenings we dance here
in the old sewing room
i sing the blues for him when he's tired and achey.
he fears i love him
i fear i never do
and so i want to go to memphis.

my sweet brasil
will you come to new orleans?
i have told the people here about your household
and how you founded that town
on a church
a school house
and a railroad track
they find it quaint
and talk about "the country"
they do not know your own story
perhaps they might go out and see.
jeremiah and i go through manchac swamp come sunday
it is an eerie drive
pray for me that my spirit bear me up
it means a great deal for me to go
but in my soul
i am quaking still
i need your prayers
no matter what you think
brasil.

dear brasil
what's wrong?
never visit the enemy in her camp?
believe those hen-stories about new orleans?
or is it me?
jeremiah eats soup like an old man
and you sit in judgment
from half-day's distance   ·
how dare you keep silent like this
you know i need words
i expected better
and who are you
to pass judgment on me?

dear brasil
last night i woke up singing
only to discover the door locked
from the other side
i believe it is the first time
but how can i tell?
mostly i never leave this room
once i come in here
i just sit
looking out at the date palms
or aunt titia's face
flying on the ceiling
i seem to believe she was missing a limb
no one ever said
but i seem to believe it so
is that why they locked the door brasil?
brasil
was it your doing?
did you write and tell them you had heard from me?
and just think
last night i sang every song i ever knew
in the whole wide world.

dear brasil
my head
opened down the middle
to the left-hand side
is a crokersack
filled with broken nut shells
and sassafrass leaves.

dear brasil
jeremiah has lost all control
and papa jac won't speak to me
except to blame me
brasil
i know you are out there
in the world
they try to keep me from you

by explaining that you are not
they say you have not been since 1897
is that so?
and all this time
you let me go on believing
encouraging me even
to sit in this very boudoir
telling you the details
of all my intimate thought and being?
papa jac even pulled out his bible the other day
and pointed to the date
what is that to me?
ciphers on paper
all but gone to dust
they say if i can admit what they call the truth
that i will really be alright
by that i suppose they mean
hanging up crokersacks
and sucking soup from cracked bowls.
i suppose they mean
i will actually go out to that churchyard
and look at a slab of concrete
they want me to believe is you.
how can i tell them
that all along,
all along i have known that you
are unfinished rock
hard
precious on the downside
from lying so close
to the earth?

2.

my voice is an okono drum
and my throat is its dance

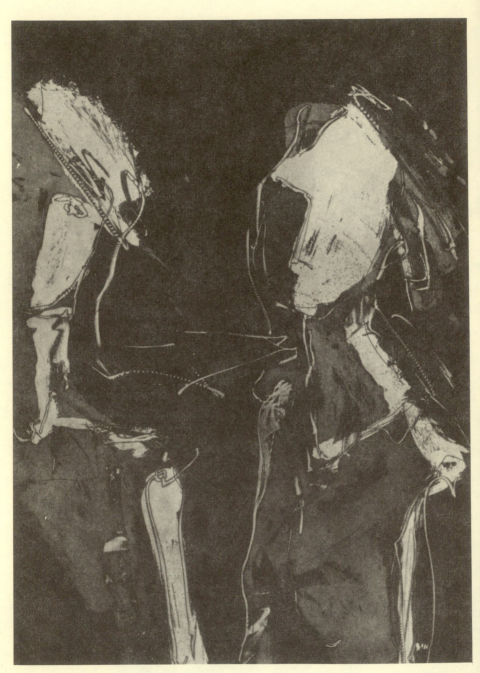

Etching by Colette Delacroix

LIVING IN THE TAN HOUSE

1.
what did percy jerome mean
marrying me
and locking me up in that big block of wood
on calliope street i never will know
but he's dead
and i can't say it matters now
i got my godchild marie steel
to come up here and live
watch me and the house just in case
she's about as good as they come
just stays in church is all

2.
he came from off tennessee street
that was before i knew him
in the back of my mind
i guess i must have wanted him even then
but there is talk
and so you keep silent about such things
until someone else
brings them to your notice
so i suppose i wanted him
those years he was living round aunt gert
before i ever knew of him
or at least
that's what he said
once he'd come to court me

somehow i never understood
that it meant we would marry
everyone said that was foolishness
and what did i know —
a girl of nineteen
knowing what a grown man of thirty-seven should do?
we married then

and two years later
he bought this unsightly house
and had it painted tan
people coming into the neighborhood looking for me
the old folk would say
"lavinia, miss thierfield's daughter?
she's living in that tan house up the street"
finally that was how everybody called it
"that tan house"
and so did i
after time had passed

3.
things went alright
percy jerome treated me good
took care of the notes
but i needed something
i really did just need something
i tried to tell percy jerome
but all he could figure
was having a baby
like having a baby was supposed to do something for me
and when he commenced to talking like so
i set him straight
and learnt all over again
to make do without words
but i still needed something
and when i would go out late of a night
and work my garden
it was like i could feel this something
pulling me
just pulling at me from down under the ground
and that was how i discovered my throat
and commenced to singing
people'd say
"lavinia, ms. thierfield's daughter,
we never knew she could sing before"
they never did
because i never did

till one night my throat opened up
and i commenced to singing
it was like hearing a language that never had been
it was like having a whole other woman
standing in your middle
singing out your insides
and to tell the truth as i know it
i still cannot find the words

4.
my voice is an okono drum
for sacred rituals
this whole city i move in
moves to the left
two steps at a time
to the songs i declare

5.
mr. p. c. ubain moved next door to us
five years later
he was an old gentleman from point-à-la-hâche
he collected bits of thread from people
was making this tapestry thing
which he called history
old p. c. ubain didn't bother a soul
except to get his cuts of string
he would step out his backdoor
to hear me singing at night
he said nothing at all
i could see him through the hidden-lily
and i knew he was listening
mr. p. c. ubain was listening at me

6.
this song has no words
i am singing this song
from a place i have not known
i am singing without words
i need to say those things
for which no words are coined
my soul is a rice field
and this voice
ancient hum
first waters
first darkness
original somniloquy
for my soul is laid down.

ELIZA

there is a mirror in the hall chiffarobe
where eliza stands
when she is five
seven
twelve years old
it holds something that pulls at her
something she can not hold
has not yet learnt
to touch

put your hands on your hip
and let your backbone slip
eliza's mother calls her inside
and puts her hair in tiny braids
if this yard is not big enough to hold you
then stay inside, child
i want you never to go over there again
hear me well
little girl

her hipbones protrude
she runs her hand over one
in a furnished apartment she lives in
on alexandria
he brushes her hand away
replacing it with a kiss
i want you never to leave me
he says
as she moves to the mirror

on a front porch in louisiana
it is easy to consider
flip sides of children's
flat breasts and behinds
eliza goes inside
to wash her mother's hair

why you always had to bother
with that miss clothilde
i'll never fathom
her mother's head is in the sink
covered in blue and green foam
your hair is so beautiful mama
while it's drying
i'll go on over to tea

i doubt seriously that tea will scald
you've stirred it full five minutes
i won't ask you about your mama
i'm sure she's fine
it's your sass in coming here
holds my mind so

i wanted to see you
was all she said
couldn't i just want to see you

what have you done
eliza
i want to know what you have done
child

the little suisse biscuits
are short with butter
they fall away from the roof of her mouth
eliza stirs them about with her tongue
looking out toward the date palms in the neutral ground
she is thinking of the seedy fruit
that makes her stomach
fall together
it's called cleaving
she says aloud
when things fall together that way
and stay
it's called cleaving

there are things
ms. clothilde
i say to no one
sounds i never rehearse
moving between corridors
way in me
i am not hiding
but there are some things
i never let out
these biscuits, ms. clothilde
i think
are quite dry

if you had moving around in you
what i have in me
your mama would have you
locked up in some convent
close to the waters
what is better eliza
to have them keep you moving
or to have them
throw you down flat

i must keep moving
this body is a fever
i must needs burn out
i must keep moving
or be floored by a movement
i can not see

is it the dark
i hear him asking
but all i tell him is
i can not sleep here
and then i see his eyes
like tamarind seeds that night
should have waited till he was asleep
but i was lying in the damp
and he clove to me

standing before the mirror
my hips are axe-heads
ready for work
smooth and easy
yet so hard to handle
i should have waited till he was asleep
i should at least have waited

i must keep moving
i must keep moving
put my hands on my hips
what have you done
what have you done
i was in that damp
and he clove to me
locked up in a convent
close to the water
he clove to me
hips and backbones
before the chiffarobe glass
i will learn not to
i must keep moving
i will learn not to
let
it
slip.

EILEEN

1.
in the middle of the kitchen floor
eileen stood stoop-shouldered
moving only her eyes
slowly
with much effort

i could kill me somebody

was all she said
and afterwards there were dead people
lying about the linoleum
taking turns
not looking dead

2.
for five days she told no one
the sixth day
she went out into the middle of onzaga street
and said

you all come
help
i have done killed my people

like pie-man telling out his pies
you all help
i've done killed my people
and they been dead near on a week

3.
perhaps she never thought they would come
never expected them to help
or even believe

and it is such a lonely sound
early in the morning
a voice calling in the streets
trying to peddle off dead bodies to the neighbors
but they never quite caught on
and so eileen went back into the house
to wait for the law
and the law came with plastic bags
scooping up miss dotty
and miss martha
and little julienne and doreen
the law scooped them up into plastic bags
and called next of kin
to clean out the mess
eyes and noses
thick portions of flesh
eileen they said
in her grief
sat stock still
and would be months and days
recovering from the shock

4.
a year or more went by
eileen stopped wearing black
and then
the neighbors began to be afraid
eileen could be heard
all hours of the night
not what she said
but her voice
her laughter
empty and stark
a hungry laugh it was

5.
in the mornings she would greet them genteelly
meet them at market
ask after their people
touch the children's hair
and after dark
when she was alone
in the little shotgun on onzaga street
she would stand before the mirror

i could kill somebody, she'd say
and laugh like anything
like nothing at all.

TOKEN STONES

the rose-hip tea is cold
but i drink it because she does
because i am afraid to change the subject
even though no one is telling anything
her eyes are peach stones
rose petals
anything but eyes to me
i think she will touch my hand
but of course she does not
she needs no foreword
talks in vertical lines

in 1919 gilbert julien had me put in infirmary
all he said was he couldn't help me none
and anybody could see

what i needed was help
if they hurt me or not in there don't matter
but it marked me when i come out
julien came to meet me
brought me back here to my house
i never said a word on the wagon
but i could tell he'd been in here
nothing was unclean or covered
he knew what day and all
but i never thought julien would do that to me
he loved me so
nothing ever told me
he would have me locked up
sometime i'd try to think what it was
but then that drove me so
it was like being whipped all about the head
he was as gentling as could be when i came home
and i would find him looking at me
from a doorway or a corner without no lights on
the next part of the year
we was sitting on the divan one day

and he said he loved me like always
that did it
i told him i didn't know nothing of that kind of love
and when he said he would go to lafouche
to see his people
i told him i wouldn't want him coming back

gilbert julien would write me
and i would write him back
but he never got my letters
i never mailed them
they sat around forever on the coffee table
or stuffed in the armchairs
and i believed it would be years
before i would say my own name again
or leave this house
for years i would sit here
with my hands on my knees
and my head would just hang
listening to the way the house sounded
in all that quiet
i never did come to understand
what made gilbert julien
put me in that infirmary in 1919
and i was no more than a girl

i was just a girl
carrying around this heavy thing in me
like somebody had put a ready-made house in me
and i had to carry it around like a lunch pail
only it come to no use to me
but in 1926 i found these
bertha left them for me years ago
i found them in the china closet
and then it didn't matter no more
not infirmary
not gilbert julian and his love
it didn't make a difference
because i had these
it didn't mean a thing no more
do you see, girl?

i think she asks me twice before i can look at her
those peach stones between her eyelids

i am sitting at my dining room table
the edge gone off my feelings
i am holding the token-stone she gave me
i am thinking it may be years
but i know it makes no difference
at all

RAMONA VÉAGIS

in 1916 ramona véagis fell off the side of the world
she filled the bathtub to overflowing
and sat down in a kitchen chair
in the middle of the water.
when miss lucille and mr. eddy did knock through that door
there was water everywhere
and the children had to be sent outdoors.

they always said she went off that way
on account of them not letting her marry lejean
except i remember when ramona véagis come to me
and told me
said she had fallen off the world
and could not climb back on

2.
it is done this way
i am quite sure this is how it's done
you run around and around
the circumference of your world
so fast
that you can not possibly fall off
still there is some secret
i seem to have forgot.
help me ms. regina
i know you ought to know,
help me stay on my world
or else there is no one i can go to

3.
ramona véagis come up these front steps
like it was a thing she done all her life
and when she looked up at me
out of all that écru
and that feather hat
i could see in her forehead
all the lights and shapes that child had broken into
like jewels of shattered crystal
on the sitting room parquet

4.
in the morning before day
i used to wake up in a clutter of voices
i should have known
i should never have trusted them
or maybe i told lejean
he was still coming for me in the evenings then
so maybe i told him
and maybe that was why
but saturday before last
everything shifted
mama lucille hit me across the back
with a dustmop handle
and that was the first thing
that was how i took to my bed
it was nothing lejean and his people put on me
it truly wasn't
mama struck me with that mop handle
and i took to bed
and when i woke up that evening
and she was sitting there so worried
that was the third thing
when i bit her in the face
and saw the purple blood run down
that was when
because before then
i truly was quite safe
i never thought i'd come here ms. regina
i never thought because look
how did i know i should commence
to falling off the world
all of a sudden
now?

5.
ramona véagis come here
looking for me to give her roots
looking for me to moan and step over her
for me to heal her
and knowing i could not,
i'm sure she knew
even when she first came
her eyes
coming out of all that écru
said i was not to blame
said all i could do
was to sit with her into evening
watching her hands
rise and fall
with my white lace curtains
blowing up over our heads
on the little settee

6.
ms. regina can not help me
she can not break my fall
i am moving way too fast
to be caught up in even a chamy bag
i speak these words
in one of many voices
and already
even now
the world from which you hear me
is so many fallings from my sphere
i have fallen so fast
you will think perhaps
you do not hear me calling
at all
1

3.

...together
they will witness the history
and hand down the tale...

Etching by Colette Delacroix

74.

CHIFALTA

1.
kiss me
here
she said
right here
in the center
of my hand
why do you hesitate?
those are only
blues
what are you
afraid of?
that you might not
die
if you
struggle somewhat?

2.
there was a catalpa tree
quite alone
among the other trees
the heavy
mottled
flowers
fall easily
with the slightest breeze
and do you think
i have spent all this time
sheltering myself
building this outer hull
only to be drawn in
like the rest of them?

3.
they are lonely
they are lonely
they bend over in semi-circles
grovelling after their own insides
unable to touch
even themselves
someone should show them how easy it is
to touch their own bellies
head to center
arms encircling
in easy
spherical
motions
i have done so
i have done so

4.
mother
mother
the catalpa tree will die
it is folding itself
it is afraid to bear flowers
mother
mother
the catalpa tree is bending
it is folding itself
and afraid to bear flowers

why are you calling me
why are you calling me
i was shucking oysters last evening
and i heard you singing
what do you want of me?
all i have
is sayings
and pearls

5.

in a dream just now broken
beneath the catalpa tree
i kissed her palms
and rolled into a song
of weary
purging nightcalls
when i awaken
she is laughing
i have done so
i have done so
mother mother
i have done so

6.

i am no longer sure
what struggling is

7.

go away from me
chifalta
i can not bear your madness
and my own as well.

WRITING THE WORDS

"It was not Death, for I stood up,
And all the Dead lie down—"
from Emily Dickinson, No. 510
1862/1891

i stand here
solitary
nearly weightless
in a room of white walls
and lean, dead men
these are only shadows
of endless histories
randomly attached to me
for the sake of simply saying
this is
or has never been
no one listens to words anymore
and how are we to hand down the tale?

sally's body
was the very signature of pain
mohab never loved her
once her stomach turned to rock
he said it was the smell of beer he hated
everyone knew it was a toddy she had
before turning in at nine
but mohab could never love her
after her belly turned to stone
and her hair fell out
the only thing left to value of hers
was the fine handiwork she could do with a needle
other folks used to do no more
than stitch

who will put the history down?
even the devil's children
once listened to words.

sometimes
i am this lone woman
standing in a field
where only weeds
survive
realizing that i also
will never be a flower
but at least i know
that i am soil
could a sally ever see me
as soil?
i plant words
and bring up myself
even if no one sees me
i can be the history of migrations
coming up through city pavements
reminding them of where home
really is
even if i am only
the dirt washed off turnips
by old crusty-faced women
surviving in settings
where even wild parsley
can not grow.

who will set it in time?
what happened
to reading by candlelight
after the lights are shut off?

mohab is praying
sally
sally
mohab is praying
where have you gone?
where have you gone?
the night is time
the sky gives witness to history
over in the rice field
with embroidery thread
and gilt-tipped needle
i can see sally
stitching her bald head
to the back of her womb
mohab is praying
sally
mohab is praying
and i am witness
and when i can no longer testify
i will stitch open my eyes
i will stitch them to my fingers
and together
they will witness the history
and hand down the tale

sally

FLYING SOLO

she began to speak
first
of the old ones
the mothers and grandmothers
wearing silk scarves
and hooped earrings
the ones who appeared dressed up
in flat sandals
and broomstick skirts
and covered their heads
to go to church
and pray
when there was no shame
for suicides
of sisters and friends
it only meant their bodies
could not be carried
before altars
except in the longings
of sisters and friends
equally afraid
to die in hunger
or the fear of it

i was giving
was all she said

i remember

she is teaching me
even now
she is shutting out the possibility
of ever forgetting
the wild
growing thing
fighting to breathe
in soil that is either too damp
or too dry
she reminds me
that when i was five
it was my ambition
to be a bird
it was my destiny
to soar
the sound of gas is like that
a soaring
a moving out

it is a solo flight
and you may take no one
with you.

THE FÉFÉ WOMEN

and i am dangerous now
i have seen the féfé women
coming out a long ways in the distance
their feet are telling
all the lives
you could not ever bear to know
the féfé women will tell you
then leave you on your own
like a death wagon
turning down bolivar street
greeting you with its mournless heap
crossing your field of vision
without a single backwards glance
without apology
or undue pause
the féfé women are like that
known not for mercy
but for grace.

BIOGRAPHIES

BRENDA MARIE OSBEY, author of *Ceremony for Minneconjoux*, attended Dillard University, Université Paul Valéry, and the University of Kentucky. A native of New Orleans, she has taught French and English at Dillard University. Her poems have appeared in *Obsidian, Essence,* and *Callaloo.*

* * * * *

COLETTE DELACROIX, whose art work appears on the front cover and in this volume, is a New Orleans artist. Her etchings in this volume are parts of her "Untitled Night Scene #1" (24" x 36") and "My Fond Memories of the Dead" (18" x 24").